THE MAGICAL
AMULET BAG

by

Sigrid Wynne-Evans

Computer Illustrations and Layout
by Lori Berry

Wynne-Evans, Sigrid, 1956-

The Magical Amulet Bag/by Sigrid Wynne-Evans
ISBN # 0-9648360-1-7

CREDITS

Once again, I could not have written and published this book without a lot of help from some very good friends.

Lori Berry — Thanks for the quick job on the computer work and illustrations.

Ralph Allen — for the great photos. You have the patience of a saint and the skill of a master.

Linda Benmour — Thanks for the constant encouragement and support, editing and photo layout help.

Milton Firestone — for your input and keen eye.

Kim Osibin — for your ideas and laughs. (By the way — she makes the most fantastically beautiful Goddess and Mermaid lampworked beads I've ever seen. Call her at (415) 472-6070 if you're interested.)

And of course to **Jasmine**, who is always there when I need her. I couldn't ask for a better daughter and friend.

Dear Beaders:

Thanks for your letters and encouragement to continue with my work. It is fantastic to know that I have found friends all over the country through my beadwork. I love to hear from all of you.

If you'd like to write or send me comments as to what you like (or don't like) about my books, or if you need some help because something is unclear, please write to me at the address below. Please send me a SASE for reply. I do try to answer ALL letters.

The question I receive most often is "where can I get beads?" If you need supplies and don't know where to get them, buy "The Bead Directory." Send $18.95 plus $3.75 shipping and handling payable to:

The Bead Directory
P.O. Box 10103
Oakland, CA 94610

This is *THE* sourcebook that is a MUST for every beader.

HAPPY BEADING!!

SIG

Sigrid Wynne-Evans
The Beaded Bear
P.O. Box 110894
Campbell, CA 95011

(408) 379-8647

TABLE OF CONTENTS

INTRODUCTION

Amulet bags have become quite popular in recent times. Perhaps it is because the bags are a connection with an era long past. Amulet bags were once the carrier of special powers and protection, the contents of which were only known to the owner. Or perhaps it is because of the elegance and the ease of self expression that these modernized amulet bags allow the maker. Whatever the reason of the popularity of the amulet bags, they are a joy to make and an even greater joy to wear.

Most of the patterns that I have seen for beaded amulet bags are geometric designs. I like the challenge, and the results of a picture in my beadwork, as those of you who've bought my earring pattern books know. The construction of the bags in this book is very simple, there are no fancy shapes or fancy stitches to worry about. The exciting part of the bags in this book are the patterns themselves.

I hope that you will have fun making the bags in this book. Be daring and creative with the finishing touches. If you wish to have matching earrings to wear with your new bag, refer to my earring design books. You will find that most bags will have a complimentary earring design in one of my earring design books.

THE BASICS

There are few materials needed to create the bags in this book. The choices of beads and beading supplies that are available are vast. The correct choices will make the bags beautiful, while the wrong choices may make the bags less than appealing. Therefore, I will attempt to give you a bead primer in hopes that your choices will help you make an amazing bag.

NEEDLE AND THREAD

The easiest choices that you will have will be the type of needle and thread that you will use. Most of you will choose to use a size 11^0 bead (more about bead sizes later). For this size bead, a size 12 beading needle will do just fine.

Beading needles differ from regular sewing needles in that they are longer and thinner. The eye is narrow and long as compared to a sewing needle. This is an important feature in that the holes in beads are fairly small and you will be passing the needle and thread through the bead more than once.

Beading needles are available in several sizes. Size 12 is the most commonly used. A size 15 needle will be needed for size 14 beads. As with beads, the higher the number, the smaller the diameter of the needle.

"NYMO" beading thread is highly recommended for any type of seed bead work. Do not use regular sewing thread as it has a tendency to fray much too quickly. "NYMO" thread is a nylon thread which is fairly strong and is available in several sizes. My personal preference is to use size O or A. Other beaders like to use size B, which is thicker. Since some Czech beads have quite small holes, even in size 11^0 beads, the B thread may fill up the beads in the base row so that you will not be able to pass through the beads for the completion of the fringe. Therefore, I use the smaller size thread to ensure that I will be able to pass through the bead several times.

Many beaders like to wax the thread with bee's wax. The wax will help keep the thread from fraying and knotting. I do not wax my

8

thread. Again, this is just a personal preference. I do not like the waxy feel of the thread. Sometimes the wax also builds up on the top of the beads. The wax also adds bulk to the thread which may be just enough to fill up the hole of the bead so that you won't be able to pass through the required amount of times.

While I have given you my own personal preferences as a starting point for your choices of needle and thread, I do not mean to imply that other choices are wrong. Try other choices to see if they work better for you. There really is no single right way, only what works best for you. So experiment!

BEADS, BEADS, AND MORE BEADS

Now, we have reached the fun part!! And also the most difficult in terms of the choices that you will have available to you.

Seed Beads are the basis for the designs in this book. Bugle beads and the small 4mm crystals may be used at the end of the fringe as accents. There is a wide array of seed beads available. A basic knowledge of the different types and styles that are available will help you with your selection of beads for the bags in this book.

Seed beads are packaged for sale in many different ways. Some stores will package beads in small tubes, others will sell them by the hank. On occasion you will also see seed beads packaged by weight. How these beads are sold often depends on how the supplier distributes the beads. So, if you are comparing prices, about the only fair way to compare price is to know the price per kilo or per gram.

Seed beads come in different sizes, the most common sizes are 9^0, 10^0, 11^0, 12^0, 13^0, 14^0, 15^0 and 16^0. Of these, 11^0 is the most widely used. Remember, the higher the number, the smaller the bead.

When working the designs in this book, bead size uniformity is very important. Beads will vary in size within a hank and from manufacturer to manufacturer. I've used 11^0 beads that look more like 10^0, and 11^0 beads that look more like 12^0. Care must be taken in choosing beads!

Size 11^0 will work well for the designs in this book. If you are a beginner, then I would recommend that you start by using size 11^0, simply because you will have more to hold on to. However, I strongly recommend that you use Delica beads. They will make your bag absolutely beautiful.

The number one rule of buying beads is to buy all the beads you will need (or can possibly buy) of the style/color that you intend to use. If you favor certain colors, it may be in your best interest to buy bulk (1/4 kilo or more) because unless you are very organized and lucky, you will either forget where you bought those beads, or the dye lot has changed, or the worst of all possibilities — it is a discontinued color/style. This has happened to me several times. Also, the bead import business or the reliability of the manufacturer may be such that your favorite store is out of that particular bead and it may take 6 months for them to get another shipment.

So, enough about size and on to style.

Seed beads can come in a variety of cuts. Smooth beads have been tumbled to give their surface a regular texture. There are no facets. These are probably what you think of as the typical bead.

Cut seed beads can be found as 2-cuts, 3-cuts, and hex-cuts, with facets on 2, 3, and 6 sides respectively.

Charlotte beads have little facets cut into them on 1 or 2 sides. These beads reflect the light very nicely and can give your piece a very elegant look.

Seed beads also come in a variety of finishes. The most common ones are listed below:

Aurora Borealis (AB), also known as **Iris, Iridescent**, or **Fire Polish**: These have a rainbow effect on the surface.

Ceylon: Surface is some what pearlized.

Delica: A laser cut bead in wonderful colors. Highly recommended.

Greasy: This is an "old" finish. It's opaque, but has depth. The colors are very limited. Yellow, turquoise, and green are the most common.

Opaque: Light will not pass through these beads. Sometimes these are referred to as chalky colors.

Transparent: Light passes through these beads, giving your piece a stained glass appearance.

Beads To Beware Of!!!!

Metallic beads look so beautiful. They shine so beautifully and are spectacular in a piece. But alas, how they fade!!

I've used some metallic Czechoslovakian beads in a beautiful fuchsia and a brilliant blue. The bags were spectacular! But two days in the sun made them fade from those lovely colors to wishy washy colors with strong tin color overtones. In short, a disgusting color that no one would like.

Japan is manufacturing some lovely metallics that I've been seduced by. Before I use them in a major project, I'll test them by leaving them out in the sun and by washing them to see how they hold up. Rumor amongst those in the know is that they do last provided that you don't shower with them or use them in areas where perspiration and body oils will degrade them.

Surface dyed beads are another problem bead. If they aren't marked as such, the give away signs are: a mottled appearance on the surface of the bead (uneven color) or the holes will have a tendency to be a tad darker than the surface. I've had some poor quality beads that were pretty enough in their package, but the color rubbed off during the course of working with the piece! Pinks are especially prone to this. So keep your eyes open to this problem.

Color lined beads may also be a problem. These beads have a different color painted in the hole from what the outside color is. Sometimes this inside color can rub off.

CHOOSING COLORS

I have provided a color code for each design in this book. The color codes are only a suggestion or a guide. These colors have worked well for me, but if you wish, try other colors.

From the above discussion on beads, you can see that if the code calls for a "RED" bead, you will still have to choose what type of "RED" bead to use. The choice of color and type of finish of the bead can make or break the design. With the simpler designs, involving 2-3 colors, the choice of beads may not be as critical. Beads with a reasonable contrast will almost always work. However, on complex designs involving 5 or more colors, particularly when 2 or more shades of the same color are used, contrast will become critical.

One of the first lessons in creating designs that are identifiable is that if several colors of transparent beads are used together, they tend to blend in together. For example, light pink with white or pink with lavender. Since the success of the design will depend heavily on the distinction of color changes, you will not want a blending of colors.

When choosing colors, generally I will choose colors that are as distinct as I can possibly find. If you choose your colors by laying hanks of beads together, you may be surprised to find that even if the hanks contrast well, if you were to place one or two beads of each color together, they may be nearly indistinguishable. Always put one or two beads of each color together on a needle if there is any question of whether or not the beads will hold their own distinct color or if the eye will blend them together. This is especially important for transparent beads, although some opaque hues may need this test as well.

Transparent beads are wonderful for background colors, especially if opaque colors are used for the design. Light will pass through the transparent beads making them recess into the background, while the light will stop or reflect back to the eye on the opaque beads used in the design. This type of contrast is strong. Areas requiring a strong definition such as outlines should almost always be done in opaque beads.

AN EXTRA TIP

Uniformity of bead size will always be important. The design and shape of the bag is affected by the beads in it. If all beads are not of a uniform size, it will be instantly noticeable. When looking at a hank of beads, you will notice that there is some variation in size. Some may be fat while others may be slivers. Try to choose beads that are fairly uniform.

THE CRAFT BUSINESS

One day many of you will want to venture into business selling your beadwork. When I first began, I had no idea of how to go about selling my beadwork. It took years of research and many hard knocks to learn what I know now. I will give you a few ideas on getting started so that your start won't be as much as a struggle as mine was.

There are several ways in which to sell your beadwork. The most common ways are: 1.) direct sales, such as wholesale and retail; and 2.) consignment. Each of these has endless possibilities.

When you are first starting out, consignment is probably the first opportunity that will come your way. Consignment means that the store will keep your merchandise and will pay you a percentage of the selling price after the piece has sold. Most seasoned craftspeople will not take on consignment accounts because there are some very definite drawbacks. But for the beginner, a consignment account may be a very good opportunity to sell beadwork provided that certain pitfalls are avoided. The main thing that I want to impress upon you is that the store has no risk in consignments. So if you agree to consignments, be sure that YOU set the terms, because if anyone loses it will be you.

Consignment agreements will vary from store to store. Consignment agreements may be 70/30, 60/40, or 50/50. The first number is the percentage of the sale that you will get, the second number is the percentage of the selling price that the store will retain. Be sure to find out if the store will add on their commission to your asking price or if they will subtract their commission from your price. Depending on the answer, you may have to adjust your prices accordingly.

With consignment accounts be sure that you get all the specifics in writing. Have everything spelled out such as: when you will be paid (after each sale or monthly), who is responsible for theft or damage (don't sign the agreement if the store assumes no such liability), what percent of the selling price you are to receive, and how much of a notice will be required of you to pick up your work if you wish to reclaim possession.

Another way to sell beadwork, and in my opinion, a more fun and profitable way, is at Art and Craft Shows. There is a significant investment required before you can participate in a show as you will need to acquire an acceptable display, i.e., canopy, tables and possibly a display case. In addition, some show fees are expensive. The advantage in participating in the shows is that you are selling at retail cost rather than at wholesale, and the potential for repeat business as well as custom work is high. Also, you may get calls for your work from someone who picked up your card long after the show is over.

Before participating in a show, visit the event to try to get a feel for how well attended it is and try to get an idea if your work would be well received with the clientele. If you're lucky enough to find a beader at the show, try to see if she (he) is willing to share some information with you. While some people are rather tight lipped about the whole process, others are more than willing to try to help.

A word on pricing — a general formula used by many crafters is: Wholesale Price = cost of materials x 3 + hourly wage. While this is a guide, it is not the end all in pricing. Most people forget to consider costs such as gas and time to go to stores to buy supplies, storage equipment, packaging or cards for displays and many other incidental costs. With all things considered, a beaded bag may only cost at most $15 to make, perhaps the most important consideration is the time involved.

I am a rather vocal advocate of beaders getting paid for their artistry. Few of us actually do. Yet there are some beaders who give away their work. This is what angers me. I've seen some beaders who've made my designs and sold them for about $40. I know the time involved. DO NOT SELL THEM SO CHEAPLY!!! My wholesale prices for most of my bags range from $85-$150 depending on the complexity and the type of beads and accents used. My retail prices range from about $150-$250 on most bags. If the store tells you that you are too expensive, then you have not found the right market for your work. Keep looking!!! Those of you who sell too cheaply do a great disservice to the rest of us, and reinforce the idea that beadwork is a "CHEAP" form of art.

NETTED AMULET BAG DIRECTIONS

BASE ROW CONSTRUCTION

1. Begin by constructing a row of 40 bugle beads. (This is the same technique as the base row of the Comanche weave earrings.)

Pick up two beads and slide them down towards the end of the thread (I like to leave about a 6 inch tail for finishing). Then go **up** through the first bead only and pull tight. This will bring the beads side by side.

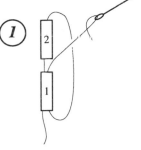

Pull tight

Now go **down** through the second bead. This should leave the beads looking like this:

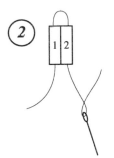

With your thumb and index finger, hold these two beads closely together and make sure that the thread is tight! Pick up one bead and go **down** through bead number 2 and pull tight. Notice how you are following the direction of the thread? Think of making full circles, with the needle and thread. You now have 3 beads side by side with your thread coming out of the bottom of the second bead.

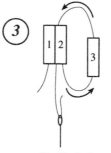

Pull tight

Before you can pick up another bead, you must always have the thread coming out of the last bead. So now go **up** through that 3rd bead.

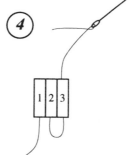

Now you can pick up another bead. Bring the needle and thread once again **up** through that last bead and pull tight. Remember, think of making a full circle whenever you add a new bead!

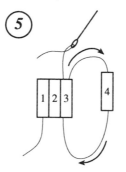

Bring the needle and thread **down** through the last bead.

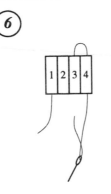

Continue, repeating Steps 3-6.

Hopefully, you are seeing a pattern emerging. Your needle and thread are following a circular motion. Always follow the direction of the thread. Continue in this manner until you have the required number of beads for the base row.

NETTING STITCH FOR NETTED BAG

2. Pick up 40 beads in a dark-light-dark-light combination (20 of each color).

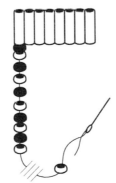

3. Bring the needle up through the 4th dark bead from the bottom.

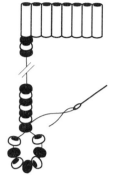

4. Pick up 3 beads (light-dark-light). Go into the 2nd dark bead as shown. Continue this sequence until you get to the top dark bead.

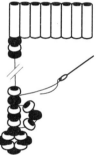

5. Bring the needle up through bugle #2, then down through #3. Pick up dark-light, then through a dark bead as shown.

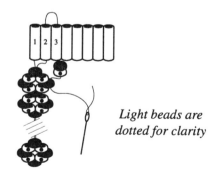

Light beads are dotted for clarity

6. Continue picking light-dark-light combinations and going through dark beads of the 2nd row as shown.

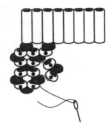

7. When you come out of the last dark bead, add 5 beads as shown, go up through the next dark bead.

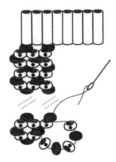

You will notice that the dark beads of the descending row stick out a bit further than the rest of the other beads. Continue picking up the light-dark-light combination, going through each of the dark beads which stick out. Finish the row by going up bugle #4 and down #5. Continue until the end of the bugle row.

8. Once the netting is complete, fold the bag in half. Stitch the side seam by lining up beads from each side, sewing them together in a zig-zag manner.

The bottom of the bag is sewn together by linking the dark beads together. This is almost like a zipper effect. These beads are also the beads from which the fringe hang from.

9. The fringe is attached to the bottom of the bag, by going through the dark beads.

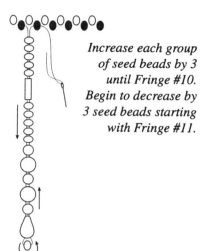

Increase each group of seed beads by 3 until Fringe #10. Begin to decrease by 3 seed beads starting with Fringe #11.

FINISHING TOUCHES FOR THE NETTED BAG

1. Add a dangle or charm from the top of the bag:

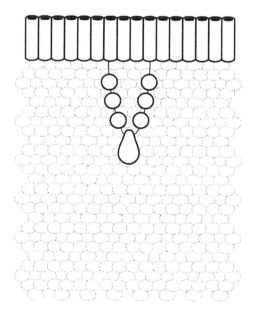

20

2. Sometimes, no matter what you do, some thread shows at the top of the fringe. You can hide this by making a "skirt." This also softens the bottom of the bag. (Note the difference in the photo between the two netted bags.) Add the skirt after the fringe is done.

Method 1

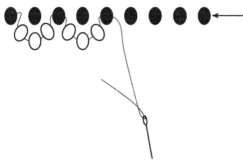 *These are the same beads that the fringe comes out of.*

Method 2

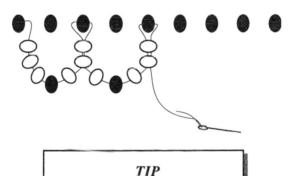

TIP

To keep thread from entangling in the fringe, wrap the fringe in tissue. It will save you a lot of time untangling thread from the fringe!

These "skirts" also work well with the peyote stitch bags.

PEYOTE STITCH DIRECTIONS

Note that the patterns at the end of this book show *only* the *front* of the bag. If you wish, the pattern may be repeated on the back. I leave the back a solid color and "sign" my bags by stitching in my name. I have provided graphs of letters so that you may do the same.

The "start" number given on each graph is the *total* number of beads you need to pick up in order to begin that particular bag. These beads are both row #1 and row #2.

READING A GRAPH

In order to follow a graph, you must understand how to read it. Note how the rows are numbered.

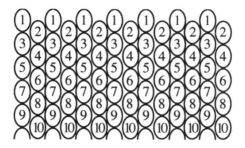

Thread a needle with about 1 yard of thread. Thread is used single strength. Begin by picking up the number indicated on the graph. (Remember that when beginning a peyote stitch bag, the start number of beads is both row #1 and row #2. Single bead stitching begins with row #3.) If you are a beginner, and do not wish to follow a graph, pick up 30 beads of one color. Tie the beads into a circle by running the needle through the beads from beginning to end.

Now we begin with the single bead stitching. If you are following the pattern, pick a spot on the graph to begin with. Mark that point with a dot. Pick up colors accordingly. For beginners, use a second color for row #3.

Put a bead on the needle, skip one bead of the circle and go into the next. If you are new to this, it helps to say to yourself "the thread is coming out of bead #1, skip bead #2 and go into bead #3. Continue until you have reached the end of the row.

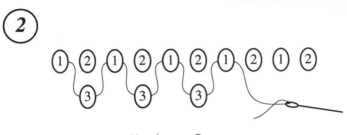

Numbers = Row

You have reached the end of the row when you go into the same bead as this row started out of.

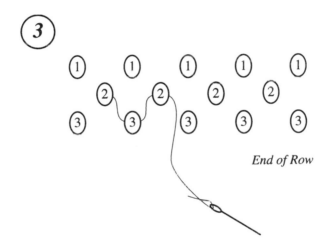

End of Row

At this point, you are now ready for the "step down" into row #4. Bring the needle (do not pick up a new bead) through the first bead of row #3.

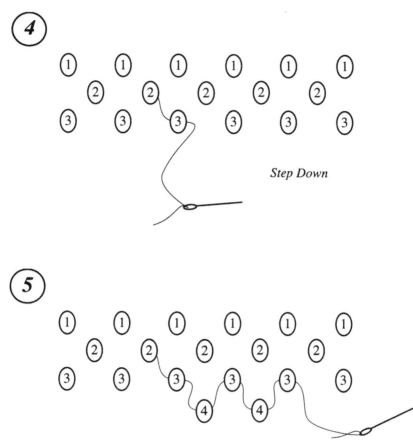

Step Down

Starting Row #4

This step down will occur at the end of *each* row. You can sew the last bead of a row and step down in one stitch once you are comfortable with this technique.

Note that by the nature of this "step down" that the first bead of each row will be one bead to the right of the first bead of the previous row (if you work from left to right).

Since a lot of people like to use "supports" for the work, I feel that I should at least mention them. If you wish, you can make a support to fit inside of the bag by using a toilet paper roll and adjusting the size by cutting and taping the roll. Some like to use a support because it provides an aid to hold the work. I personally find the support to be cumbersome and it is just another item for my thread to get caught up in. Whether you use one or not is your own personal choice. If you do choose to use one, make one to fit the bag after you have completed about 4 rows.

A cylinder will form as you are beading. If you have chosen not to use a support and you are using Delica beads, you have an option as to whether you would like the bag to be round or flat. If you choose to make it flat, simply center the pattern and squash the beads flat. This will also give a very well defined edge to the bag which should have an edging stitch to make the bag look finished. Regular round beads will not flatten as the Delicas will, therefore an edging stitch will not be necessary.

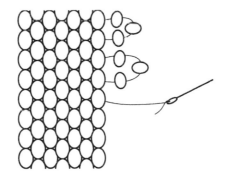

Once the bag is finished, stitch together the beads of the last row in a zipper-like fashion.

FRINGE OPTIONS

Fringe is optional on the amulet bags, but fringe gives the bag such style. For me, making the fringe is my favorite part of making a bag. It is such fun choosing beads and charms to use in the fringe that it's easy to get carried away.

As with the chains, rather than telling you which type of fringe to use with a particular bag, I will give you options. Any type of fringe will look good on any bag.

STRAIGHT FRINGE

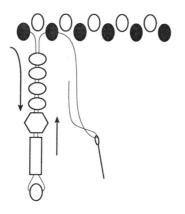

Straight fringe can all be the same length, or tapered. For a "V" taper add 3-4 seed beads to each fringe until you get to the center, then decrease.

KINKY FRINGE

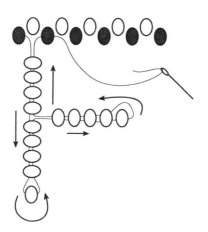

Add side fringe to the main fringe. Add as few or as many side fringe as you like.

LOOPED FRINGE #1

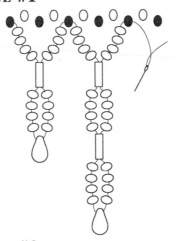

LOOPED FRINGE #2

Begin by connecting center beads and work outward. It will be easier to gauge the length of each loop.

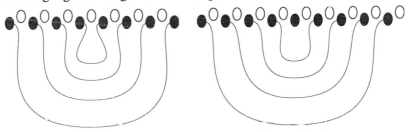

Even number front   *Odd number front*

LOOPED/STRAIGHT COMBINATION

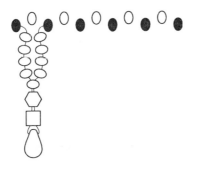

The top part of this fringe is a loop. The bottom portion is straight. Use large beads on the bottom portion and seed beads on the top.

Daisy Chain Fringe

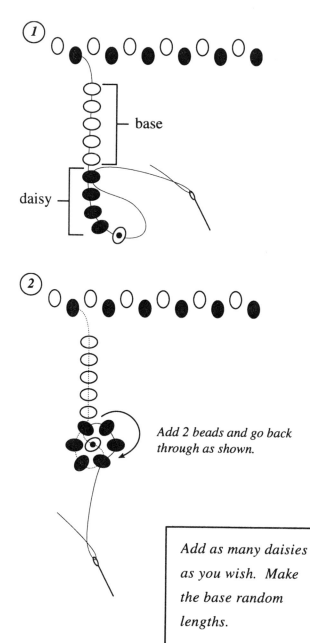

base

daisy

Add 2 beads and go back through as shown.

Add as many daisies as you wish. Make the base random lengths.

STRAP OPTIONS

SINGLE STRAND STRUNG BEAD STRAP

Attach a double thread to the top of the bag. String beads as desired and securely attach thread to the opposite side of the bag. Attach another double thread to the bag and re-thread all of the strap beads for re-enforcement.

❑ Try stringing a pattern of 4 seed beads (11^0) and one 6^0 seed bead.

❑ Add accent beads such as crystals and fetishes.

MULTI STRAND STRUNG STRAP

Attach a double thread to the top of the bag. Add a combination of 10 seed beads and one accent bead. Secure thread to opposite side of the gab once the desired length is obtained. With a new double strand of thread, pick up 10 seed beads and go through the accent bead. Repeat to end. Add as many strands as you wish.

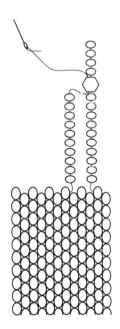

FIGURE 8 STRAP

Attach 2 threads to the top of the bag (double strand). Pick up 4 beads with each needle. Bring right needle through the 4th bead of the left side, and left needle through the 4th bead of the right side.

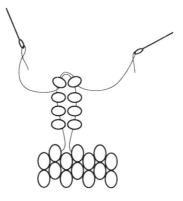

Continue by picking up 4 beads on each needle and crossing over until you've reached the desired length.

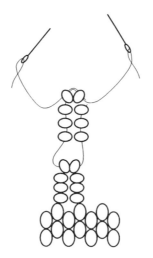

For the last group of beads, pick up 3 beads with each needle and connect to the bag. Weave through several beads for security before knotting.

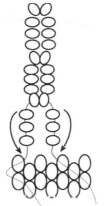

PEYOTE STRAP

Peyote stitched straps are simply an extension of the peyote stitched bag. Make this strap as wide as you wish. You may also wish to incorporate patterns.

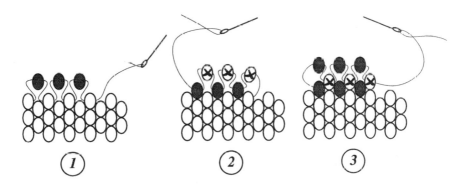

3-COLOR DIAGONAL STRAP

Make this strap on its own. Attach both ends to the bag after the strap is completed. Use single thread.

① Pick up ●○○●⊗⊗.
  Tie in a circle.

② Add center ●.
  Pass through ○.

③ Add ⊗⊗○.
  Pass through lower ●.

④ Add ●○.

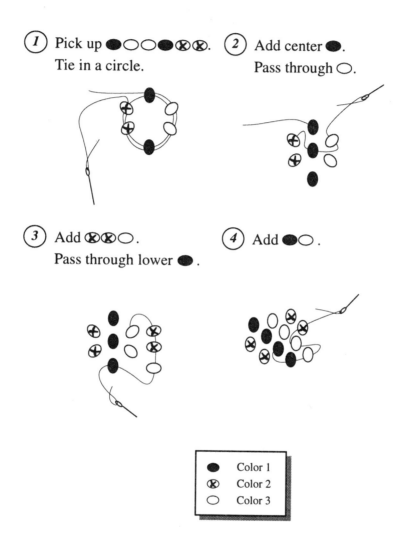

●	Color 1
⊗	Color 2
○	Color 3

Amulet Netted Bags

1. Peace
2. Sun & Moon
3. Basket Weave

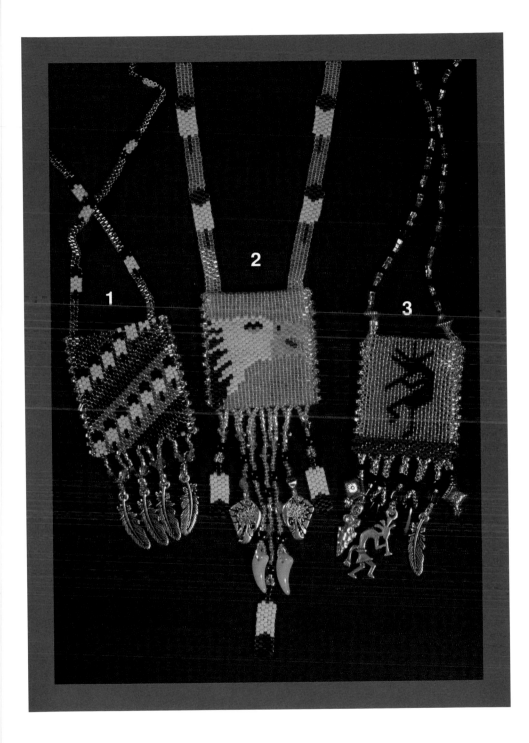

1. Feathers
2. Eagle
3. Kokopelli

1. Mermaid
2. Fish

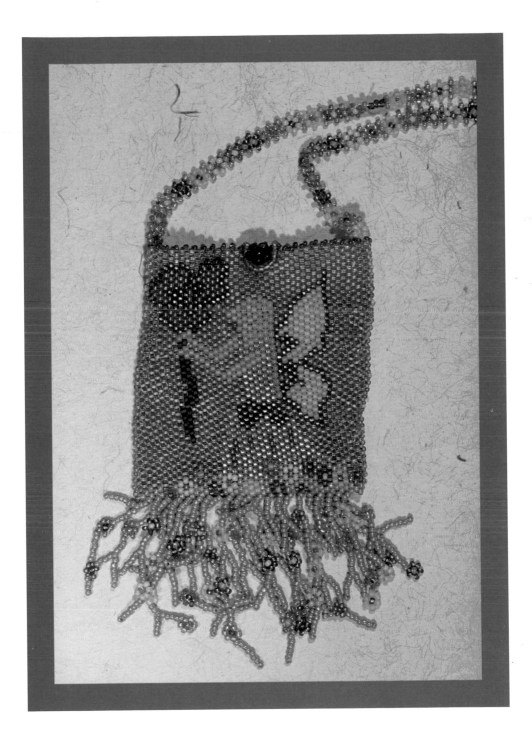

Flower Fairy

1. Goin' Fishin'
2. Jaguar

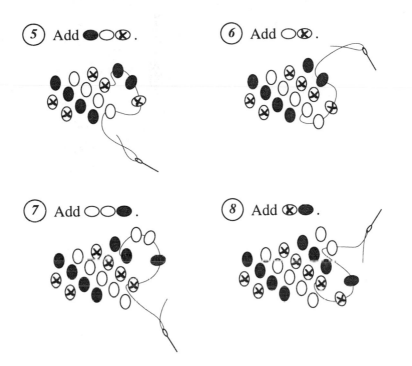

(5) Add ●○⊗.

(6) Add ○⊗.

(7) Add ○○●.

(8) Add ⊗●.

Repeat steps 3-8 until you have reached the desired length. Connect ends to the bag by sewing securely.

DAISY CHAIN STRAP

① Tie 6 beads in a circle.

② Add center.

③ Pick up 2 beads of the next daisy. Stitch as shown.

④ Pick up 4 beads to complete circle.

⑤ Add center.

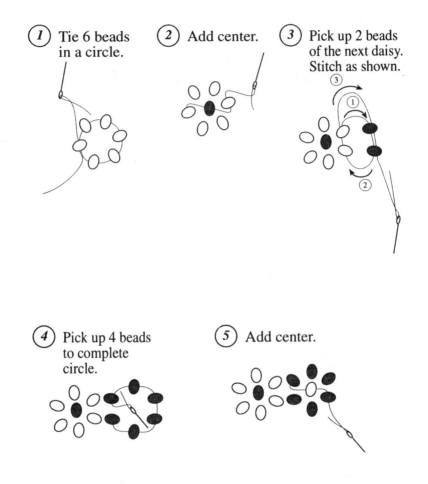

34

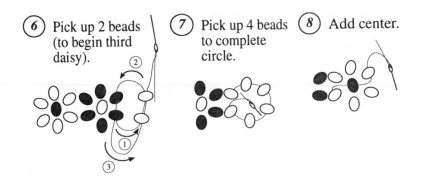

6 Pick up 2 beads (to begin third daisy).

7 Pick up 4 beads to complete circle.

8 Add center.

Repeat steps 3-8 until you have the desired length. Make daisies in as many colors as you wish.

CLOSURE FOR PEYOTE STITCH BAGS

A closure is not necessary on these bags, however, if you would like one, it is easy to add.

LOOP/BEAD CLOSURE

You may need to extend the top of the bag so that the bead (button) used for a closure does not interfere with the design.

Sew a bead 6mm or larger on to the front top of the bag.

From the back, form a loop of seed beads large enough so that it can go over the bead in front, snugly. Reinforce several times for strength.

PEYOTE PATTERNS FOR AMULET BAGS

As a reminder, these patterns show only the front of the bag.

The 'start' number is the total number of beads you need to pick up to begin the bag.

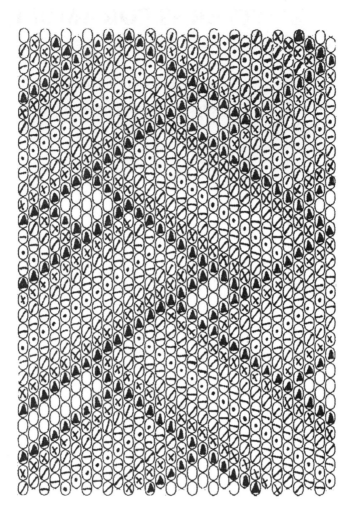

Start: 60 beads

Basket Weave

▲ Dark Green

✖ Medium Dark Green

✦ Medium Green

━ Pale Green

• Very Pale Green

◯ Blue

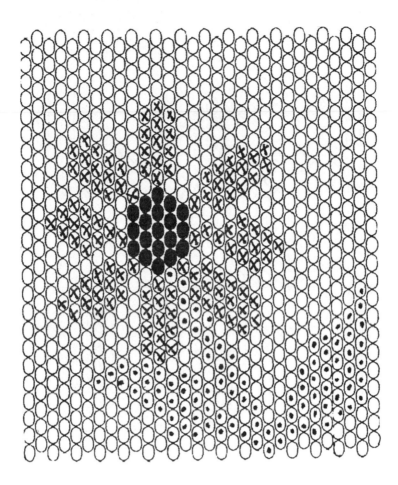

Start: 30 beads

<u>Daisy</u>

✖ White

● Orange-Yellow

· Green

○ Blue

39

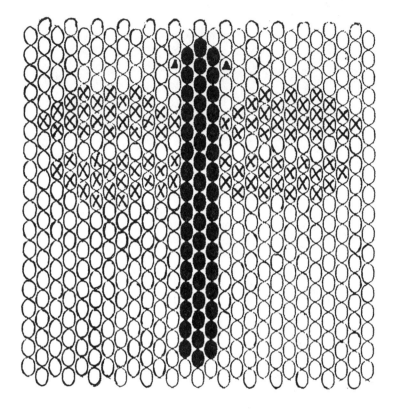

Start: 54 beads

Dragonfly

● Black

✖ Transparant Light Blue

▲ Orange

◯ Bronze

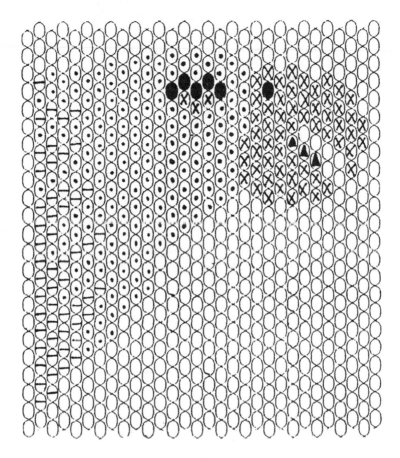

Start: 60 beads

Eagle

—   Brown

·   White

●   Black

✗ Yellow

▲   Red

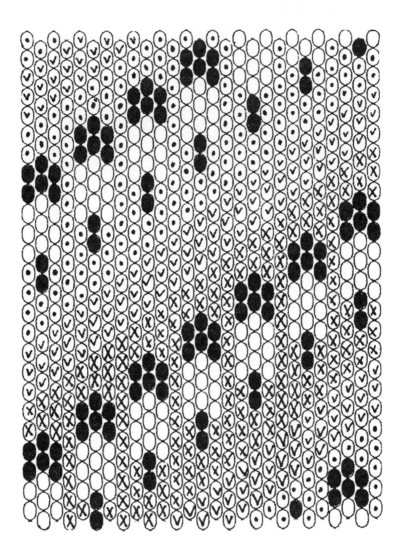

Start: 54 beads

<u>Feathers</u>

- ⚬ White
- ● Black
- ✖ Turquoise
- ˅ Pink
- · Grey

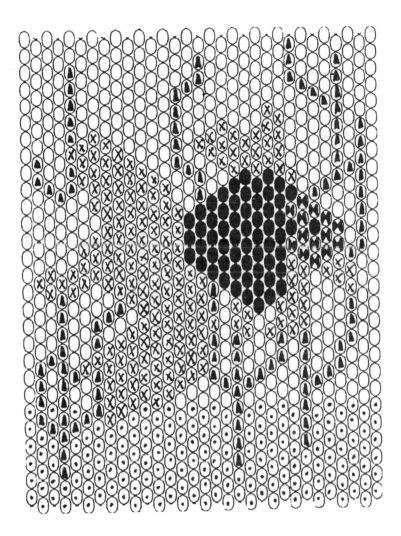

<u>Fish</u>　　　　　　　　　*Start: 62 beads*

- •   Sand
- ○   Transparent Blue
- ✖   Bright Pink
- ●   Purple
- ⋈   Yellow
- ▲   Green

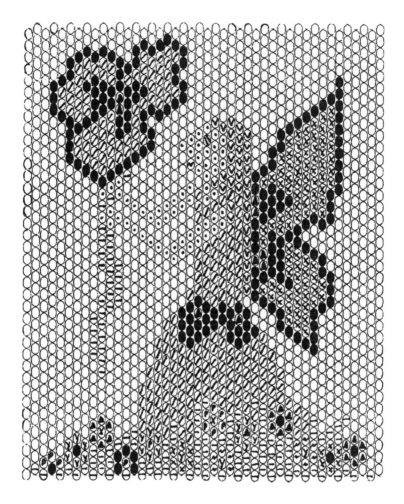

Flower Fairy

Start: 88 beads

●	Purple	＼	Blue
╱	Violet	✖	White
•	Flesh	ρ	Pink
⌄	Yellow	Υ	Gold
—	Green	○	Lt. Transparent Blue
▲	Orange	∿	Red

44

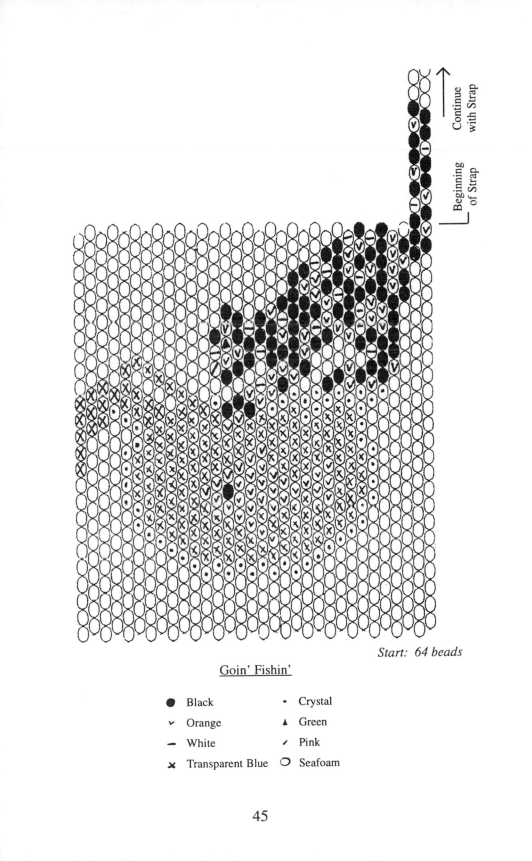

Continue with Strap

Beginning of Strap

Start: 64 beads

Goin' Fishin'

- ● Black
- ● Crystal
- ∨ Orange
- ▲ Green
- — White
- ╱ Pink
- ✗ Transparent Blue
- ◯ Seafoam

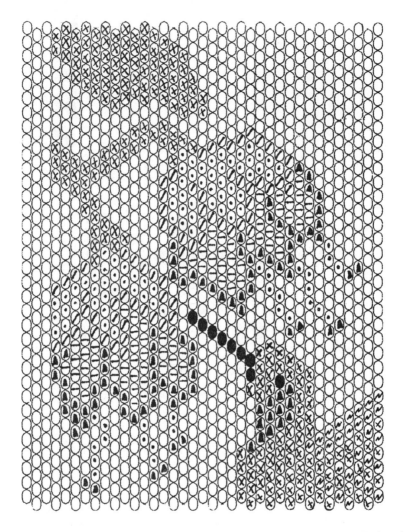

Start: 74 beads

Hummingbird & Fuchsias

✖	Green	—	Pink
✔	Purple	●	Black
•	Lilac	∿	Dark Green
▲	Bright Pink	○	Light Blue

46

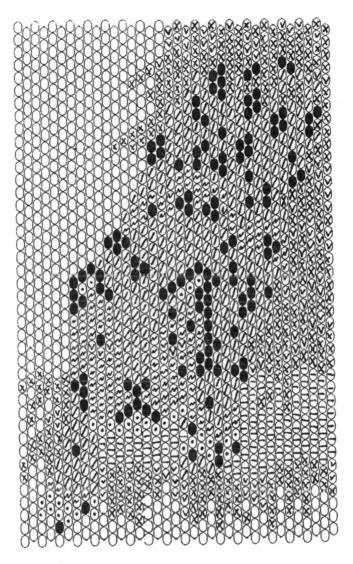

<u>Jaguar</u>   *Start: 72 beads*

- ∾ Orange
- ⁄ Tan
- ⌄ Light Green
- ✕ Dark Green
- • White
- ○ Transparent Blue

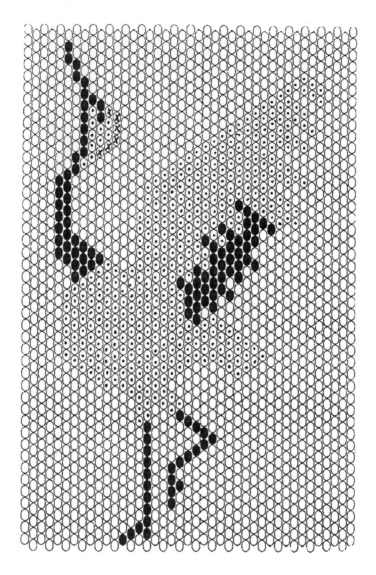

Start: 82 beads

Japanese
Crane

- ● Black
- · White
- ✖ Red
- ⬭ Gold

48

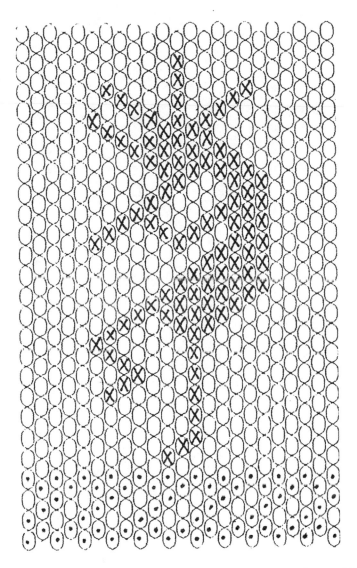

Start: 46 beads

Kokopelli

✗ Matte Black

◯ Silver

· Matte Red

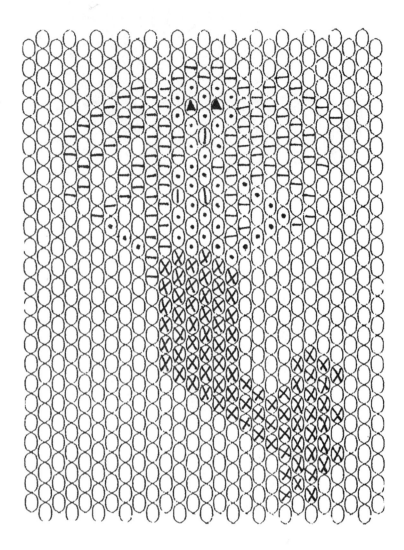

Mermaid   *Start: 54 beads*

- — Orange
- · Flesh
- ✖ Green
- ❙ Pink
- ▲ Light Blue
- ⟡ Dark Blue

50

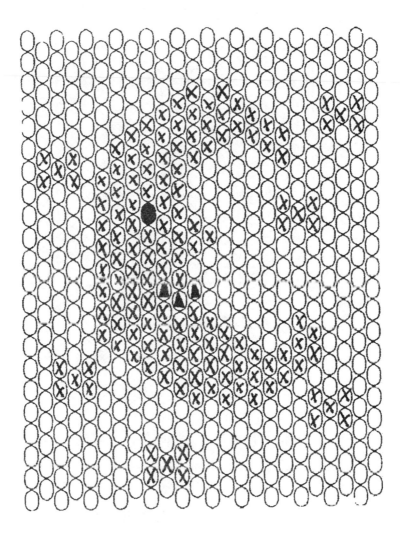

Start: 48 beads

51

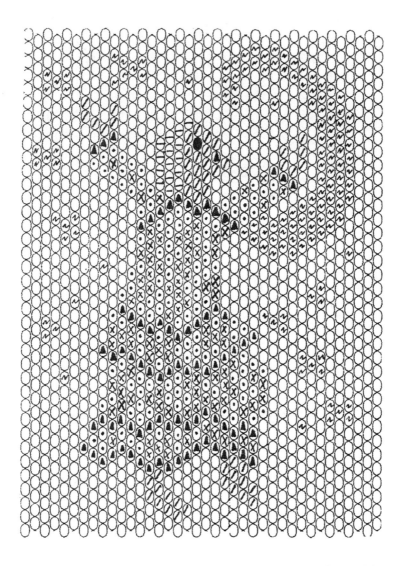

Start: 76 beads

Moon Dance

✓	Flesh	•	Purple
▲	Red	○	Midnight Blue
—	Brown	∿	Silver
●	Blue		

52

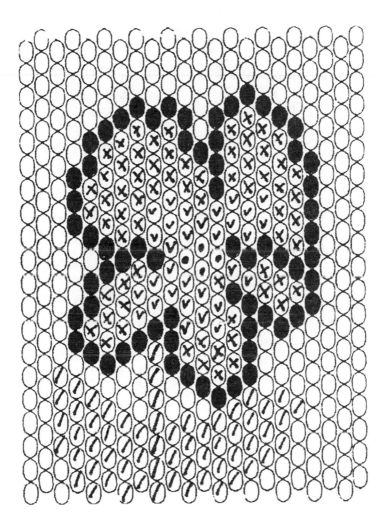

<u>Pansy</u>

Start: 44 beads

○ White

● Dark Purple

✘ Lilac

˅ Orange

• Yellow

✓ Green

53

<u>Peace</u>

Start: 42 beads

- **✗**   Red
- **/**   Orange
- **•**   Yellow
- **ᵛ**   Green
- **—**   Blue
- **●**   Black

54

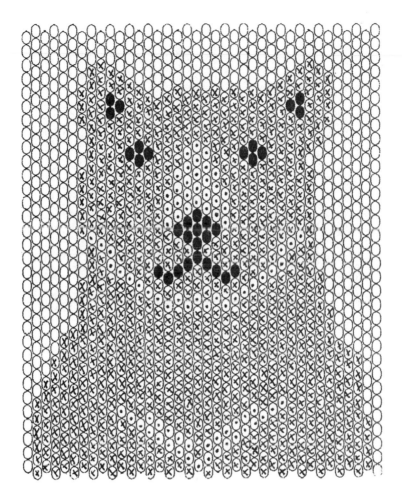

Start: 76 beads

Polar Bear

✗ White

· Grey

● Black

○ Dark Blue

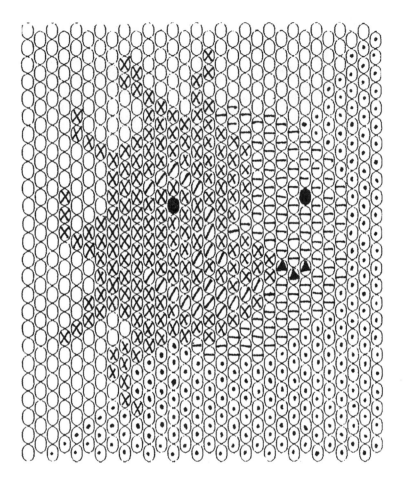

Start: 60 beads

Sun & Moon

◯	Light Blue	▲	Red
✖	Yellow	⬤	Black
╱	Orange	•	Dark Blue
─	Silver		

Start: 62 beads

<u>Tapestry</u>

- ✖ Copper
- ● Black
- ✦ Red
- • Green
- ⌃ Orange
- ◯ Purple

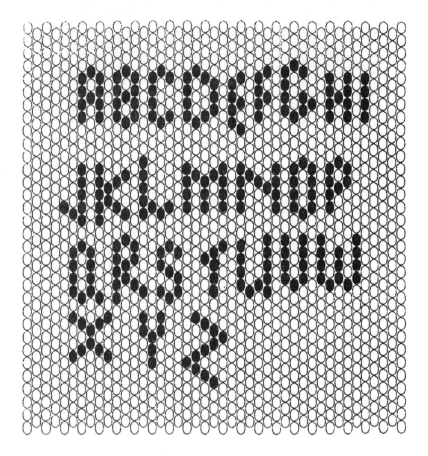

Uppercase Letters

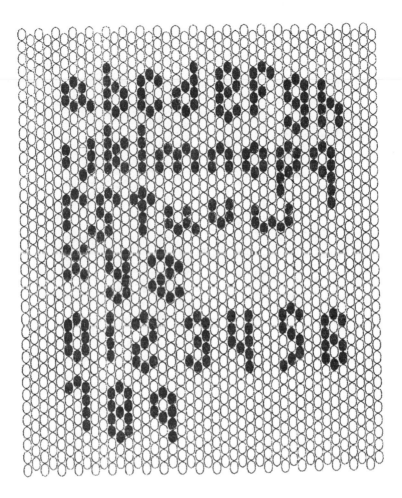

Lowercase Letters/Numbers

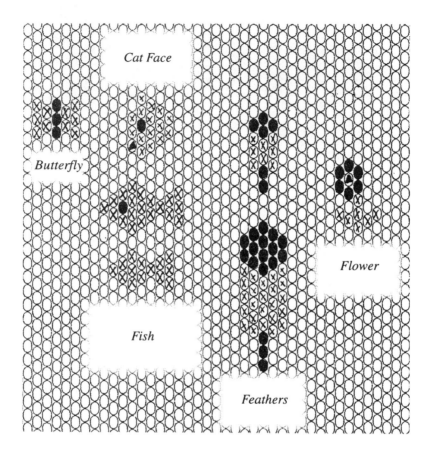

Cat Face

Butterfly

Flower

Fish

Feathers

Optional Designs for Peyote Stitched Straps

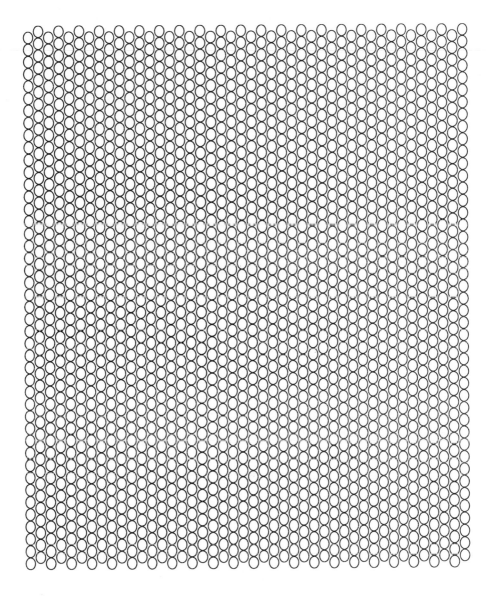

Blank Peyote Stitch Graph

NOTES

TRY THESE FANTASTIC EARRING DESIGNS!

Each book features different image designs for Comanche Weave earrings. You'll be able to find a complimentary design for most of the amulet bag designs in one of these four books.

Earring Designs by Sig Vol. 1 — Includes: Bear, Kokopelli, Cat and Mermaid.

Earring Designs by Sig Vol. 2 — Includes: Eagle, Fishes, Merlin, and Owl.

Earring Designs by Sig Vol. 3 — Includes: Angel, Crescent Moon, Santa, and Bouquet.

An Earful of Designs — Includes: Hummingbird, Fire Serpent, Japanese Crane, and Tiger.

ORDER FORM

Name: _____

Address: _____

               _____

Phone: _____

	Quantity		Subtotal
Earring Designs by Sig Vol. 1	_____	x $8.95	_____
Earring Designs by Sig Vol. 2	_____	x $8.95	_____
Earring Designs by Sig Vol. 3	_____	x $9.95	_____
An Earful of Designs	_____	x $9.95	_____
The Magical Amulet Bag	_____	x $10.95	_____

Shipping: Add $2 for 1 book, and $1 for
           each additional book   _____

CA residents must add 7.75% sales tax   _____

                     Total enclosed   _____

Please send check or money order to:

       Sigrid Wynne-Evans
       P.O. Box 110894
       Campbell, CA 95011
       (408) 379-8647

Prices and availability subject to change without notice.